For My Son

Meg Ford

DEDICATION

FOR MY SON
TYLER

You are my inspiration. Wherever your journey in life may take you, I pray you will always be safe. Enjoy the ride and never forget your way back home; I will always be here for you. Learn from everything you can, and be the great man I know you can be.

Love,
Mom

When life gives you lemons, make lemonade.

– Elbert Hubbard

ACKNOWLEDGMENTS

Thank you to my family—Rob, Rachel, and Tyler. Special thanks to our Miracle League family that has served as the Ford family church every Saturday for the last 13 years. As a coach, each team member inspires me to be better every day. This book would not have been possible without you.

⤐ CONTENTS ⤏

❧ AS YOU GROW UP ❧

For my son,

As you grow up, prepare for college, and start to live your life as an adult, I want you to remember a few things:

1. **How much you are loved.** Never forget that you always have a place to go, a person to talk to, and someone to come get you—no questions asked.

2. **Remember that college is a privilege.** Spending four-plus years learning, growing, and focusing on yourself is a gift like none other. Enjoy the journey to discover all that you have to offer the world. Never will this way come again to mix youth, freedom, opportunity, and resources together. Take advantage of everything that is offered to you. Say yes to the universe. You will have the world at your fingertips. Fill your plate with academic, social, cultural, athletic, and artistic offerings. Take it all in. Try new things.

3. **Investing in friendships now will pay you dividends for life.** Being friends in high school is easier. You sit in the same classes or do the same activities with your high school friends. Maintaining friendships takes more work as an adult and should be tended to with care. Keep in touch with a phone call, letter, text, or best of all, face-to-face interaction.

4. **I know it's hard to believe that I was eighteen once.** Few things you can say will shock me and I just may have some good advice. If you have a problem, talk with me. While the law may recognize you as an adult, you still have much to learn. I will always be here for any questions or concerns you may have.

5. **It is your good fortune that you have never lived in a place where no one loved or cared about you.** Despite the excitement of the first weeks of college, you still may have no real friends at the start, but that will change.

6. **Drinking debate.** You are at a place where alcohol is accepted and yet legally forbidden. The only thing that stands in the way of you and a bad experience is your own good judgment. Here's the tricky part: you need to exercise that good judgment at the very moment you may already be impaired by alcohol.

7. **Drugs.** When it comes to drugs, please remember, "No pills, no powder." One bad choice can have severe consequences. Pills and powders are often laced with other drugs, and you have no idea what is in them. Synthetic drugs are rampant and currently the drug "fentanyl" is leading. Fentanyl is a killer, a powerful opioid between 50–100 times more potent than morphine.[1] It can be laced in pills and powders and can even be absorbed through the skin.

---

1. https://www.npr.org/sections/health-shots/2018/12/12/676214086/fentanyl-surpasses-heroin-as-drug-most-often-involved-in-deadly-overdoses

8. **The first weeks of college are a time like no other.** Everyone will want to meet you and there will be none of the social awkwardness that usually accompanies rushing up and speaking to total strangers. Don't waste this opportunity, as it will never come again.

I have loved you every moment of your life. Even as you prepare to move on, I love you even more. This love is unconditional and comes without strings, but unfortunately life does not. When hard times come your way, motivation and perseverance will keep you going. It's important to remember that difficult times will pass. Motivation and perseverance require neither a college education nor training of any kind.

Motivation and perseverance are the same traits that will help you achieve your goals. If you are motivated to persevere, you will succeed. The way to develop perseverance is to take small steps that result in small achievements. Small achievements lead to bigger successes.

Think about creating a puzzle; you add piece by piece until you get the final image. Persistence almost always leads to success. In fact, your persistence has helped you learn to walk, talk, and write, and you have succeeded. Persistence usually means learning something new in order to achieve your main goal. Always invest in your knowledge, as it will assist you in moving forward.

Now is your time. If there are dreams you want to live, things you want to do, knowledge you want to gain, friends you want to make, and goals you want to achieve, it is now entirely up to you. You got this!

Love,
Mom

❧ YOU HOLD YOUR DESTINY ❧

For my son,

> "It is not in the stars to hold our
> destiny,
> but in ourselves."
> **– William Shakespeare**

You hold your destiny in your own hands. You can live the life you always dreamed. From here on out, your life will be defined by your own actions and thoughts. Trusting "the stars" more than yourself is a convenient way to shift the blame in case things don't work out. Life can't be lived this way. It may bring relief from the mental burden of responsibility, but only for a moment.

Optimism is the one quality more associated with your success than any other. An optimist sees challenges as temporary and as stepping stones that will lead them to a better solution. A pessimist sees challenges as permanent stumbling blocks which make it impossible to move forward. Optimistic people are a lot more fun to be around and generally lead happier and healthier lives. Believing in yourself is the first step toward success. If you don't believe in yourself, no one else will.

Your thoughts about things can have a big impact on how you feel, but it's also important to recognize that sometimes thoughts are not accurate. It's also important to understand that you are not your thoughts, but sorting them out is essential to taking the proper action.

If you are ever feeling nervous or unsure of your path . . . stop, take a deep breath, and assess the situation. By being self-aware you can be an observer of any of the symptoms that may arise from fear, anxiety, or panic, instead of being a slave to them. Noticing is key. If you don't notice, then you don't have a choice. You don't have to act in response to thoughts or feelings if you are aware of your values. It is your own actions that determine the type of life you will have. Those who have complete faith in themselves will take responsibility for their own lives.

> The fire, in the beginning, is covered
> by smoke. But in time the smoke
> disappears, and the fire
> alone burns fully.

It's now your time to burn fully on your own. Believe in yourself and trust your instincts. Learn from everything you can and take every opportunity possible. I am so proud of the man you have become and the man you are becoming. You are now the creator of your own destiny. Go forth and make your dreams a reality. I will be cheering you on every step of the way.

**Love,
Mom**

POEM FOR MY SON
(Author Unknown)

I sometimes wish you were still small.
Not yet so big, strong, and tall.
For when I think of yesterday,
I close my eyes and see you play.

I often miss that little boy
Who pestered me to buy a toy.
Who filled my days with pure delight
From early morning to late at night.

We watch our children change and grow.
As seasons come they quickly go.
But God has the perfect plan to
Shape this boy into a man.

Today my son I'm proud of you
For all the amazing things you do.
I'll love you until my days are done.
And I'm so grateful you are my son.

QUOTES TO LIVE BY

"Life is not measured by the number of breaths we take but by the moments that take our breath away."

– Maya Angelou

"Kindness should be the natural way, not the exception."

– Buddha

"Continuous effort—not strength or intelligence—is the key to unlocking our potential."

– Winston Churchill

"Success is getting what you want. Happiness is liking what you get."

– Ingrid Bergman

"Who looks outside, dreams; who looks inside, awakens."

– Carl Jung

QUOTES TO LIVE BY

"Take the first step in faith. You don't
have to see the whole staircase.
Just take the first step."
– Martin Luther King Jr

"Adapt what is useful, reject what is
useless, and add what is specifically
your own."
– Bruce Lee

"If your actions inspire others to dream
more, learn more, do more, and become
more, you are a leader."
– John Quincy Adams

"No problem can be solved with the same
consciousness that got you there."
– Albert Einstein

"The way I see it, if you want the rainbow,
you gotta put up with the rain."
– Dolly Parton

❧ LIVE THE LIFE YOU IMAGINED ❧

For my son,

> "Go confidently in the direction of your dreams. Live the life you have imagined."
>
> **– Henry David Thoreau**

It's time for you to live the life you imagined. You must believe that you are enough and have the power to make this world better. When I tell you I love you, I'm also reminding you to believe in yourself and to love who you are. I always want the best for you. And while the best may not be the easiest, you can be sure that I will always have space to encourage or comfort you along the way. I will always be your biggest fan. It doesn't matter how far away you are or how old we both become, you will always be my son.

You are my inspiration, the fire in my heart, the greatest joy in my memories, and the reason I sometimes stay awake at night and worry. I will love you on your happiest days and I will love you at your lowest points. I will love you when you break my heart. This love of mine will take on a thousand different forms, yet it will never die. I will love you for all the days of your life and beyond. Our love is eternal, and because I am your mother, our love is your foundation.

Love,
Mom

⊰ BE THE CHANGE ⊱

For my son,

> "Be the change you wish to see in the world."
>
> **— Mahatma Gandhi**

Many times we make wishes only to forget about them too soon. This happens on a recurring basis in the hearts of everyone. We have to wish less and do more. In this world, there are three categories of people:

1. Those who make things happen
2. Those who watch things happen
3. Those who wondered what happened

Those who make things happen are the do-ers. Making things happen is all about being proactive, not waiting for the next person to do what you can do. If no one wants to get it right, someone has to be bold enough to take the first step. Those who wonder what happened are those who are indifferent to the happenings in the world. Wondering what happens feeds mediocrity. Corruption, abuse, and acts of violence happen every day of our lives. If we want change, we must take the bold step to be the light in this dark world, an eye to the blind, an ear to the deaf, and a source of strength for those living with disabilities.

Improve and change what is closest to you. Many people believe that changing the world requires you to focus on making big changes. However, this simply isn't true. Many people who have changed the world did so not by focusing on changing the world, but by focusing on improving and changing that which they were already familiar with. Look at Rosa Parks, who simply refused to give up her bus seat on a segregated bus. This wasn't an act that was aiming to change nations: it was simply Rosa Parks making a small gesture because she believed segregated buses were unethical and unfair. Yet, that simple gesture changed the world by bringing more attention to the civil rights movement at the time. You have the power to stand up, speak out, and change the world.

Love,
Mom

⤳ LIFE IS A SERIES OF ⤶ HELLOS AND GOODBYES

For my son,

> "Life is a series of hellos and goodbyes."
>
> **– Meg Ford**

People are constantly coming in and out of your life. Some stay, some go, some are just passing through. Leave the door open to new people and opportunities, but don't be afraid to close the door if you need to. If someone doesn't support your ideas or your person, if they drain your energy instead of build you up, if they don't encourage you to be the best you can be, maybe it's time to shut that door. When one door closes, another one opens and it always will, because that's how life works. When people walk away from you, let them go. It doesn't mean they're bad people; it just means that their part in your story is over. Not everyone is going to want to be with you or accept you for who you really are. Accept that and move on. Your life is better when you surround yourself with people who love and care for you.

Everyone comes in your life for a reason; to teach you something, to love you, or just to experience life with you. Notice the people who make an effort to stay in your life. The people you want in your life are those that want you in theirs, make you better, make you feel alive, support your dreams, and can teach you valuable lessons. They're a source of positive energy and feedback to support the greater you. You feel positive energy or a higher vibration when you're around them. These are the people you want to keep around you. The energy, or "vibe," you feel is vital in a relationship.

Some people think that being alone makes you lonely, but I think nothing is lonelier than spending time with the wrong person or people. You cannot be lonely if you like the person you're with. Be comfortable and confident with who you are. Don't be afraid to spend time alone. If you love who you are then you don't need people to fill a void. Some people need things or certain friends to feel complete. Feel complete on your own and you will attract others congruent with your soul and life mission. If you are at peace with who you are, you don't need others to fill your emptiness. I wish you a full life of great experiences, inspiring lessons, and beautiful people that enhance your world and who you are.

Love,
Mom

⤚ DREAMS CAN COME TRUE ⤙

For my son,

> "All our dreams can come true, if we
> have the courage to pursue them."
> **– Walt Disney**

As you continue to grow and become an adult, you will live your own life, be your own person, and pursue your own dreams. You have the courage to make your dreams reality. Along the way, you will have times of great happiness and times of disappointment, but don't let that distract you from your dreams. Life has its ups and downs and it's not always fair, but I know your wit, strength, and resilience will see you through. Tough times never last, but tough people do. Never give up. Be confident in who you are and all you do. There may be hard times, but the difficulties you face will make you more determined to be who you are.

Love,
Mom

QUOTES TO LIVE BY

"Great thoughts speak only to the thoughtful mind, but great actions speak to all mankind."

– Theodore Roosevelt

"Sometimes what you're looking for is already there."

– Aretha Franklin

"All that we are is a result of our thoughts."

– Buddha

"Don't count the days, make the days count."

– Muhammad Ali

"In matters of style, swim with the current; in matters of principle, stand like a rock."

– Thomas Jefferson

QUOTES TO LIVE BY

"Courage is what it takes to stand up and speak; courage is also what it takes to sit down and listen."

– Winston Churchill

"The time is always right to do what is right."

– Martin Luther King Jr

"The great courageous act that we must all do is have the courage to step out of our history and past so we can live our dreams."

– Oprah Winfrey

"When you reach the end of your rope, tie a knot in it and hang on."

– Franklin D. Roosevelt

"And, in the end the love you take is equal to the love you make."

– John Lennon/Paul McCartney

⤜ YOU MAY BE THE WORLD ⤛

For my son,

> "To the world you may be one person
> but to one person you may
> be the world."
>
> **– Dr. Seuss**

I may have given birth to you, but you did not come with instructions. This beautiful perfect baby boy was laid on my chest the day you were born. I loved you before you were born, but once I saw you, my heart became yours. All my dreams, hopes, and love transferred to you. I knew I wanted to do everything I could to give you the best life possible. I am not perfect. I know my ineptness has caused displeasure and I take responsibility and apologize. Saying sorry means you choose your relationship over your ego. I choose us. I have made many mistakes along the way and I will make many more before I die. I wouldn't be human if I didn't. For those I am sorry. Understand that they come from me not knowing and not from lack of love.

I love you and support you no matter what. You are loved for the boy you are, the man you will become, and the precious son you will always be. Sometimes when I need a miracle, I look into your eyes and realize I already created one.

Love,
Mom

❧ AS YOU PREPARE FOR COLLEGE ❧

For my son,

As you prepare for college, it may feel like a whirlwind with a lot coming at you very quickly. You may feel like everyone else knows what they're doing. (They don't!) Remember, you are ready for this. You've been preparing all your life and you are ready for college. You are not only ready, but highly capable of a successful and a wonderful life.

In times of confusion, anxiety, or utter panic . . . stop, breathe, assess the situation, and only then move forward. In all my years in college, I found when I didn't understand what was going on or I felt like the professor left something out, if I went back and carefully re-read the syllabus, the course materials, or the directions, the answers or the timing would be there. Asking for help from others works, but always consider the source. Keep in mind what you "think" you know (or heard, or read) may be very different from what is expected. I feel confident that the college you choose will be a good fit for you, but that is for you to determine. Give it some time as you find your place. It doesn't all have to happen at once and most likely it won't. College will open your already curious mind to new ideas and ways of thinking. You are already a fun and engaging person to talk to about complex ideas and subjects. I can't wait to have even deeper conversations with you about the things you will learn, the projects you will work on, and the friendships you will make.

Hopefully, your dad and I have done a decent job up to this point of guiding you toward adulthood. I have some simple advice for you about living on your own:

1. Eat regular healthy meals.
2. Make your room your place of sanctuary; you will need it.
3. Take time for yourself to re-energize if you are feeling overwhelmed.
4. Get enough sleep. Good sleeping habits are part of good health, but don't rely on sleep aids.

5. Schedule your time wisely and don't procrastinate. Writing deadlines on a calendar (not just your phone) is a good way of keeping track of your commitments.

6. When you drink (and we are assuming at some point you will), be very careful about with who, what, where, when, and how. Don't mix alcohol. Being shit-faced drunk is about as pathetic as it gets, and please don't post pictures of your experience on social media unless you want to live with it forever.

7. Have fun and make lots of friends. Don't jump into other people's drama too quickly. You have the good sense to be able to spot people that aren't worth your time or energy. But at some point, they will sneak under your radar. Be measured and careful about who you trust and who you confide in.

Going to college is the next step for you. If it feels unfamiliar that's because it is. You have already taken hundreds of new and unfamiliar steps along the way. You are well-practiced in the art of moving forward and have shown that you can do it successfully. You should give yourself credit for that. It is a life skill that not many your age possess.

We are proud of you. This is an exciting time of your life. It's an exciting time for us too, watching you grow and navigate life as you become an adult. Sometimes it may be overwhelming and scary, but if you can power through and stay focused, you will be fine. This is a new beginning for you. The path won't always be clear. Listen to your heart and dreams and sense of what is right for you. I believe in you and all that you are. If you need anything at all I am always here for you, no matter what. Enjoy the ride. There are amazing things to see along the way, incredible people to meet, and life-changing experiences ahead. If you are lucky, you will continue to grow, evolve, and get to know yourself better. Wherever your journey in life may take you, I pray you will always be safe. Take it all in, enjoy yourself, and never forget your way home.

Love,
Mom

TALENTS
NO TEST CAN MEASURE:

- Your kindness
- Your artistic ability
- Your creativity
- Your growing independence
- Your ability to work in a team
- Your compassion
- Your ability to express yourself
- Your ability to make and keep friends

TALENTS
NO TEST CAN MEASURE:

- Your problem-solving skills
- Your design and building talents
- Your musical ability
- Your ability to love
- Your inspiration
- Your dedication
- Your generosity
- Your happiness
- How much you are loved

QUOTES TO LIVE BY

"Well done is better than well said."
– Benjamin Franklin

"If you are not willing to learn, no one can help you. If you are determined to learn, no one can stop you."
– Zig Zigler

"It always seems impossible until it is done."
– Nelson Mandela

"Done is better than perfect."
– Sheryl Sandberg

"Every accomplishment starts with the decision to try."
– John F. Kennedy

QUOTES TO LIVE BY

"In the middle of every
difficulty lies opportunity."

– Albert Einstein

"Nothing is impossible.
The words itself says I'm possible."

– Audrey Hepburn

"No legacy is so rich as honesty."

– William Shakespeare

"Little minds are tamed and subdued by
misfortune; but great minds rise above it."

– Washington Irving

"I've grown most not from victories, but
setbacks. If winning is God's reward, then
losing is how he teaches us."

– Serena Williams

MEN ARE WHAT THEIR MOTHERS MADE THEM

For my son,

> "Men are what their mothers
> made them."
> **– Ralph Waldo Emerson**

The relationship between mother and son is a special one. A boy who is loved and cared for by his mom turns into a confident man. This relationship is imperative for overall development and emotional health of a man. When a man shares a strong relationship with his mother he gains a lot, as it directly affects his relationship with his future spouse. A man who loves and respects his mother, also loves and respects his wife. Happy marriages are associated with warm and secure mother-child relationships.

I am your foundation and you are my gift. It will remain throughout time and distance. It is the purest love; unconditional and true. It is the understanding of any situation and forgiving of any mistake. I am always here for you and I love you no matter what.

Love,
Mom

❧ WITHOUT STRUGGLE THERE IS NO PROGRESS ❧

For my son,

> "Without struggle, there is no progress."
> **– Frederick Douglass**

Struggles teach us lessons and make us understand our strengths and what we are capable of. This, in turn, makes us stronger when facing any challenge we come up against in life. Surviving difficult times gives you the confidence to continue to learn, grow, and evolve. The fruit you reap after struggling is the best and sweetest compared to the ones you get without much effort.

Struggle is essential for a person to value what they have. You know the real value of money when you earn it. It's the struggle that adds a sense of worth. It's the daily struggle of the farmers that allows you to eat. Undergo each struggle with the intention of learning new things. Don't see struggle as something which brings you down or gives you pain. See struggle as a new opportunity. Nature gives you struggle to learn a lesson. This short story explains how struggle can be crucial to carrying out your life goals:

A man spent hours watching a butterfly struggling to emerge from its cocoon. Though it managed to make a small hole, its body was too large to get through it. After a long struggle, it appeared to be exhausted and remained absolutely still. The man decided to help the butterfly and, with a pair of scissors, he cut open the cocoon, releasing the butterfly. However, the butterfly's body was very small and wrinkled and its wings were all crumpled. The man continued to watch, hoping that, at any moment, the butterfly would open its wings and fly away. Nothing happened; in fact, the butterfly spent the rest of its brief life dragging around its shrunken body and shriveled wings, incapable of flight.

What the man—out of kindness and his eagerness to help—had failed to understand was that the tight cocoon and the efforts that the butterfly had to make in order to squeeze out of that tiny hole were nature's way of training the butterfly and of strengthening its wings. So a lot of times, it's that friction which keeps you going in the long run.

I am confident you will find your way through any friction you may encounter. I will always be here to help encourage you through any struggle (or new opportunity) in life that you may have.

**Love,
Mom**

✧ FOUR INTENTIONS ✧
FOR A FULFILLING LIFE

For my son,

What makes you happy at this very moment does not guarantee your future happiness. When you aim for a life that is fulfilling, happiness is the by-product. According to Dr. Deepak Chopra,[2] there are four intentions to make a fulfilling life:

1. **A joyful, energetic body.** Don't do anything to hurt your body. Exercise, eat healthy, and avoid toxins—that means toxic food, toxic people, a toxic environment, and toxic jobs—anything that brings illness to the body.

2. **A loving, compassionate heart.** Everybody wants love. Practice the four A's; attention (be a good listener), acceptance (don't try to change people), appreciation (notice others for the good they do), affection (care for others). Doing this is good for the heart and soul.

---

2. Chopra, D., *The 4 Intentions that Make a Fulfilling Life,* www.mindbodygreen.com

3. **A quiet, alert mind.** When your mind is reflective and alert, you have access to intuition and vision. The right things come to you at the right time without any anticipation or regrets.

4. **Lightness of being**—is living with no resistance, no anticipation, no regrets— just this moment. This is being alive, the highest experience you can have, just you as being.

Success is the realization of worthy goals— goals that bring joy to you and others. Second is the ability to love and find compassion. Third is to discover who you really are. If you follow these, everything else will fall into place. I pray you live a fulfilling life that brings happiness to you and those around you.

Love,
Mom

⤙ FAMILY IS YOUR FOUNDATION ⤚

For my son,

Your family loves you and always will. Family is your foundation to the world. They are the people that are there when you need them. Home is not a physical place, but a place in your heart. Home is where you are safe and loved unconditionally, no matter what. Typically when one thinks of families, one thinks of the traditional nuclear family with parents and children. However, a family can be made up of anyone a person considers family. Family isn't always blood related. It's the people in your life who want you in theirs. The ones who accept you for who you are, feed your soul, and support your ideas. The ones who love to see you smile and will always be there when you need them. Cherish your family; you don't know how long you have them.

Love,
Mom

QUOTES TO LIVE BY

"Happiness is not something ready-made.
It comes from your own actions."

– Dalai Lama

"They may forget what you said but they
will never forget how you made them
feel."

– Maya Angelou

"There is only one way to avoid criticism:
do nothing, say nothing, and be nothing."

– Aristotle

"Twenty years from now you will be more
disappointed by the things you didn't do
than by the ones you did do, so throw
off the bowlines. Sail away from the safe
harbor. Catch the trade winds in your sails.
Explore. Dream. Discover."

– Sarah Frances Brown

"The best revenge is massive success."

– Frank Sinatra

QUOTES TO LIVE BY

"Ask and it will be given to you; search, and you will find; knock, and the door will be opened for you."

– Jesus

"Some people feel the rain, others get wet."

– Bob Dylan

"The three essentials for happiness are something to do, something to love, and something to look forward to."

– George Washington Burnap

"The most common way people give up their power is by thinking they don't have any."

– Alice Walker

"The true profession of a man is finding his way to himself."

– Hermann Hesse

HOLD ON TO
❧ WHAT IS INDIVIDUAL ❧

For my son,

> "All I would tell people is to hold
> on to what is individual about
> themselves, not to allow their ambition
> for success
> to cause them to try and imitate the
> success of others. You've got to find it
> on your own terms."
> **– Harrison Ford**

You are the best "you" there is. Don't let anyone tell you any different. Some people in life may want to bring you down, ridicule your dreams, and challenge your person. They may look like winners on the outside, but in fact they are only expressing their own insecurities. Don't let them bring you down.

Nothing can be done without believing in yourself first. The biggest factor that will determine whether you achieve something significant is self-belief. Believing in yourself is the first step toward success. If you don't believe in yourself, no one else will. Many highly successful individuals have failed yet keep going until they achieve what they were trying to do. Their belief created vision so big that they didn't care how many times they failed. They knew they were eventually going to get where they wanted to go. And this will happen to you. Believing in yourself does not mean you won't fail. You will. But you will get up again and again. Time and hard work will get you there. The more you believe you can do better, the more you try to expand your way of thinking and push yourself to become better.

Believe and accept yourself for the amazing person you are. You never have to disrespect, insult, or hurt others simply to prove a point. It only shows how weak your position is. Loving yourself is the first step to loving others.

**Love,
Mom**

FRIENDS
⤳ ARE THE GREATEST GIFTS ⤝

For my son,

Friends are one of the greatest gifts in this life. Never take them for granted. The Japanese have the term "kenzoku," which translated literally means "family." It implies the deepest connection of friendship, of lives as comrades from the distant past. These people may have an even stronger connection to you than your own blood. Time and distance do nothing to diminish the bond we have with these friends. When you find these people, these kenzoku, they're priceless gems to be cherished. They are like finding home. They are a powerful well to drink from. Friendships are to be cherished and valued as gifts in your life. Not all friendships are the same though. There are three types of friends:

- Friends for a reason
- Friends for a season
- Friends for a lifetime—kenzoku

Friendships should encourage and strengthen who you are. Friends give us hope in the most difficult times, help to de-stress our lives and provide affirmation on life's path. Be the friend you want. What makes a great friend? Important traits of any friendship include:

1. **Trust**—This is an essential trait, as we need a friend to confide in. These friends remind you that you are not alone and empower you to be better.

2. **Empathy**—This is extremely important, as it is the ability to actively put yourself in someone else's shoes. Sometimes the best thing a friend can do is just listen.

3. **Givers**—I have found that the friends who are the most happy and positive are those that give of themselves. They are not consumed with their own problems; instead, they take action to help solve problems for others.

4. **Humor**—The best friends know how to make you laugh and are full of life and spirit. They are the ones who bring joy, hope, and comfort even during the most difficult times.

5. **Shared Interests**—Spending time with people who enjoy the same things we do allows for immediate connections and strengthens friendships.

6. **Team Players**—Putting the needs of others before yourself for a shared goal is what friendship is all about.

7. **Different Perspectives**—Friends with different perspectives and backgrounds help you grow and have the ability to transform fixed ideas or positions. Friends with new ideas, experience, and advice can help you transform into a more well-rounded human.

So, put down your phone in the presence of friends to create meaning in the time you have together. Invest in your friendships; call, reconnect, stay in touch. It's good for your overall health and your friendship. Find friends that make you feel good, affirm your soul, and who are excited about your life and ideas.

Sometimes friendships can change and fade away or end abruptly. If a friendship is not beneficial to both of you, you have the power to negotiate changes. Sometimes you may decide that it's best for a friendship to end. If a friend no longer contacts you, it's understandable to feel rejected, but you are not responsible for other people's reaction to you. If you are the friend of someone experiencing mental health problems who seems to be withdrawing from your friendship, try to understand what your friend may be going through. Their difficulties may be only temporary. Give them the space they need and make sure they know how to contact you if they decide to get back in touch. Cherish your friendships; they make life a whole lot richer.

Love,
Mom

ATTITUDES

The longer I live, the more I realize the importance

of choosing the right attitude in life.

Attitude is more important than facts.

It is more important than your past;

more important than your education or your financial situation;

more important than your circumstances, your successes, or your failures;

more important than what other people think or say or do.

It is more important than your appearance, your giftedness, or your skills.

It will make or break a company. It will cause a church to soar or sink.

It will make the difference between a happy home or a miserable home.

You have a choice each day regarding the attitude you will embrace.

Life is like a violin.

You can focus on the broken strings that dangle,

or you can play your life's melody on the one that remains.

You cannot change the years that have passed,

nor can you change the daily tick of the clock.

You cannot change the pace of your march toward your death.

You cannot change the decisions or the reactions of other people.

And you certainly cannot change the inevitable.

Those are strings that dangle!

What you can do is play on the one string that remains—your attitude.

I am convinced that life is 10 percent what happens to me

and 90 percent how I react to it.

The same is true for you.

– Chuck Swindoll

QUOTES TO LIVE BY

"Your attitude not your aptitude will determine your success."

– Zig Zigler

"It is not how much we give but how much love we put into giving."

– Mother Teresa

"It doesn't matter how slowly you go as long as you do not stop."

– Confucius

"Your time is limited so don't waste it living someone else's life."

– Steve Jobs

"Our greatest weakness lies in giving up. The most certain way to succeed is always to try just one more time."

– Thomas Edison

QUOTES TO LIVE BY

"Never ignore someone who cares for you
because someday you'll realize
you've lost a diamond while
you were busy collecting stones."
– Unknown

"An investment in knowledge pays the
best dividends."
– Benjamin Franklin

"Try to be a rainbow in someone's cloud."
– Maya Angelou

"The measure of a man is what he does
with his power."
– Plato

"Not everything that can be counted
counts, and not everything
that counts can be counted."
– Albert Einstein

✧ DATING ✦

For my son,

Dating is a tricky thing, and doing it right can be difficult but can also be fun. It is one of the most important things you will do. Because how you date will dictate *who* you date. And who you date will one day become your spouse and life partner. This is who will determine your future family, so date wisely. Here are a few expectations I have for you when it comes to dating:

1. **Always ask in a straightforward and direct way, and always ask in person.** If that isn't possible, then talking on the phone is fine. Never ask by text, instant message, or email.

2. **Always take them on a date.** None of this "Let's hang out at my place and play video games or watch a movie" nonsense. I expect you to pick up your date and take them somewhere. It doesn't have to be expensive or elaborate. Some of the best dates are simple, like a picnic at a park or a walk on the beach. You should always

make sure to take them to a place where you know they will feel comfortable and enjoy.

3. **Open the car door for your date.** Open all doors for your date.

4. **Pay for your date.** No questions asked. Your father and I will make sure you always have money for your dates if you need it. Don't ever split the bill.

5. **Walk to the door and pick up your date.** Never text from the car, or worse, HONK! And always walk your date to the door at the end of the night.

6. **Use your good sense when it comes to kissing.** Don't kiss every date, but don't be afraid to kiss the right one.

7. **Listen to your date.** The best dates involve getting to know the other person, so take your date somewhere that will allow you to talk.

8. **Always make your intentions clear.** If you aren't clicking with someone, then end it. Don't string them along. It may

hurt for a minute, but they will appreciate your honesty. And if you are feeling a connection, let them know. A date loves clarity. It will make dating a whole lot easier if you follow this one simple rule.

9. **Date around, but only seriously date one at a time.** Once you've found that special someone you are interested in seeing exclusively, be faithful. Always, always be faithful. If you decide things aren't working out or you meet someone else you'd like to get to know, refer back to rule #8.

10. **Be physical, the right way.** Hold hands, put your arm around their shoulders or eventually the waist, kiss the head, put your hand on the knee—these sweet gestures speak volumes and make your date feel cared for. Going too far, too fast physically only confuses the relationship and it can never be undone.

11. **Handle hearts with care.** Hearts are strong but they are also delicate. Don't ruin that.

12. **Get to know their friends and family** and let your family and friends get to know them, especially me.

13. **When the time comes, tell them you love them a lot.** In fact, tell your significant other all sorts of nice things. Everyone deserves to be complimented.

14. **Perform acts of service.** Make breakfast, take out the trash, and offer your jacket— you get the point.

15. **Surprise that special someone.** Again, a little can go a long way. Just stick with small surprises. Bring a case of their favorite drink or favorite candy, pick flowers, or show up at their work for a surprise lunch.

16. **Never underestimate the power of the written word.** As nice as it is to hear good things, it's even better to have them written down so they can be referred back to. You should write letters or notes to your loved one often.

17. **When the time is right and you are ready** and you've found that special someone, be sure to have a ring and get down on one knee when you ask those four special words.

I love you now, forever, and always. And I know that someday I will love her too.

**Love,
Mom**

❧ YOUR CHARACTER ❧

For my son,

> "Be more concerned with your character than your reputation because your character is what you really are, while your reputation is merely what others think you are."
>
> **– John Wooden**

A true test of a man's character is what he does when no one is watching. Your character is much more important in defining who you are than your reputation will ever be. Your character defines the person you really are. Your reputation is nothing more than what some people think you are. Eventually your reputation will become a by-product of your character. If you are of strong character, even insulting false remarks about you will be meaningless because nobody will believe them.

Another good measure of a person's character is how they behave when they are wrong. The person who when realizing that he or she is wrong quickly admits it, is a person of strong character. The most successful people don't have a problem admitting they are wrong, a characteristic that not only saves a lot of time, but enhances your reputation. Be more concerned with your character, as that is who you really are and who we really love.

Love,
Mom

10 RULES
WHEN CHARACTER IS TESTED

1. Don't worry about being right; be concerned about doing the right thing.

2. Be true to yourself. Don't let others set your standards.

3. To be trusted, be trustworthy.

4. When you're being faced with a moral decision, remember it's really your character being tested, not your reputation.

5. Toughness is a means, not an end.

6. Moral courage is more rare than physical courage.

7. If you're going to insist on your rights, be prepared to live up to your responsibilities.

8. Decide what you want written on your tombstone.

9. A good reputation may be a wonderful way to open doors, but only character will keep them open.

10. It's never too late to become the person you want to be.

QUOTES TO LIVE BY

"If you want to lift yourself up,
lift up someone else."

– Booker T. Washington

"The best and most beautiful things in the
world cannot be seen or even touched—
they must be felt with the heart."

– Helen Keller

"Failure is the condiment that gives
success its flavor."

– Truman Capote

"Happiness is when what you think, what
you say, and what you do are in harmony."

– Mahatma Gandhi

"You make a living by what you get; you
make a life by what you give."

– Winston Churchill

QUOTES TO LIVE BY

"The antidote for fifty enemies
is one friend."

– Aristotle

"Happiness is a butterfly, which when
pursued, is always beyond your grasp, but
which if you will sit down quietly, may
alight upon you."

– Nathaniel Hawthorne

"Courage is not the absence of fear but
the capacity to act despite our fears."

– John McCain

"Humility is not thinking less of yourself,
it's thinking of yourself less."

– C.S. Lewis

"The Possible's slow fuse is lit by the
Imagination."

– Emily Dickinson

✤ PRAYERS ✤

For my son,

You really learn how to pray when you have children. You won't truly understand this until you have kids of your own. Prayers.

Love,
Mom

THE LORD'S PRAYER

Our father who art in heaven, hallowed be they name. Thy kingdom come, thy will be done, on earth as it is in heaven. Give us this day our daily bread; and forgive us our trespasses, as we forgive those who trespass against us; and lead us not into temptation, but deliver us from evil. For thine is the kingdom, the power, and the glory.[3]

---

3. The Litany section of the U.S. Book of Common Prayer, 1928

THE SERENITY PRAYER

God grant me the serenity to accept
the things I cannot change, the courage
to change the things I can, and the
wisdom to know the difference.

– Reinhold Neibur

GUARDIAN ANGEL PRAYER

Angel of God,

my guardian dear,

To whom God's love

commits me here,

Ever this day,

be at my side,

To light and guard,

To rule and guide.

Amen.

A Prayer For My Son
(Author Unknown)

Your gifts are many.
I am grateful for every one.

One of the greatest gifts
is the gift of a wonderful son.

Thank you for his life, dear Lord.
Watch over him each day.

May he be safe and free from harm,
and led along life's way.

Bless him though life's trials.
Lord, may he always do what's right,

An example be for all to see as
He's guided by your light.

⋊ LIFE IS WHAT HAPPENS ⋉

For my son,

> "Life is what happens to you when you're busy making other plans."
>
> **– Allen Saunders**
>
> (Made popular when John Lennon used it in the song he wrote for his son Sean, "Beautiful Boy")

This is one of my favorite quotes. I have found that the true experience of being alive is beyond our plans and "happens to us," though this does not mean that we should not make plans. If you are depressed, you are living in the past. If you are anxious, you are living in the future. If you are at peace, you are living in the present. Anxiety, tension, and worry are all forms of fear about the future. Guilt, regret, sadness, and resentment are about the past. Living in the present means not living in the past and not waiting for the future. To stay on our path we must trust, live in the present, and let go of fear.

Living in the present means not resisting life's experiences as they happen. We are not in charge of what happens to us, but as we develop an awareness of the present moment and the willingness to experience life as it happens, our fears dissipate. Most people lose sight of the big picture and get caught up in our day-to-day lives. So, how do you change the world? Pick one thing each day that will propel you forward.

1. Never assume—after all, the future is always unknown. When you assume, you make an ass out of you and me because that's how it's spelled.

2. Opportunity always knocks, whether you are aware of it or not. When you're tired, distracted, or stressed you make more mistakes. Opportunity may be knocking, but you don't hear it through fatigue or stress. You may not recognize something terrific (or problematic) standing right in front of you. If you miss an opportunity, there will be another , just different. Even without planning, opportunity knocks.

3. Planning can be beneficial, but put it in perspective. There is no crystal ball.

Living in the present means not living in the past and not waiting for the future. Stay attentive and open your mind to other perspectives or points of view. Planning for the future is important, but so is living in the present, as that is the only time you have any power to do anything.

Love,
Mom

❧ POWER OF POSITIVE THINKING ❧

For my son,

> "When difficulties arise, the positive thinker takes them as creative opportunities. He welcomes the challenge of a tough problem and looks for ways to turn it in to advantage."
> **– Norman Vincent Peale**

Positive thinking is essential for our mental and physical health. When you let negative thoughts remain in your mind, they overwhelm both your brain and your body. Positivity is just a matter of perspective. It's your choice how you look at things. Being positive is sending out good energy and attracting great things in your life. When you are positive, you are happier. It is easier said than done, but you can train your brain. Positivity is in your mind and action. Think positive, talk positive, feel positive. When you are positive, you open up for positive energy to reach you. Think about the things you are grateful for. Try a daily gratitude journal to support turning positive thoughts into action. Health benefits from positive thinking include lower stress levels, increased life span, lower rates of depression, better psychological and physical well-being, better cardiovascular health, and better coping skills especially during times of stress. Here are some other benefits of a positive attitude:

Health: People who have positive attitudes are generally healthier.

Wealth: People with positive attitudes often are in better financial positions.

Socialization: Most people want to be around you when you're positive.

Productivity: You are more productive at school, work, and home.

Relationships: Having a positive attitude adds to the depth of any relationship.

Active Mind: Someone with a positive attitude has an active mind and they are always learning about the world around them.

We only have one chance at life in this world, so having a positive viewpoint allows you to unleash the power of life. Go get 'em!

**Love,
Mom**

QUOTES TO LIVE BY

"The ultimate source of happiness is our mental attitude."

– Dalai Lama

"We can do anything we want to if we stick to it long enough."

– Helen Keller

"Good for the body is the work of the body, and good for the soul is the work of the soul, and good for either is the work of the other."

– Henry David Thoreau

"You can't be brave if you've only had good things happen to you."

– Mary Tyler Moore

"A comfort zone is a beautiful place, but nothing ever grows there."

– Author Unknown

QUOTES TO LIVE BY

"Try not to become a man of success, but a man of value."

– Albert Einstein

"A man cannot be comfortable without his own approval."

– Mark Twain

"Love yourself first and everything else falls into line. You really have to love yourself to get anything done in the world."

– Lucille Ball

"The smallest act of kindness is worth more than the grandest intention."

– Oscar Wilde

"Yesterday I was clever and wanted to change the world, today I am wise so I am changing myself."

– Rumi

STEPS TO IMPROVE SELF-CONFIDENCE

1. Spruce up your appearance. Shower every day, brush your teeth, and run a comb through your hair. A good rule of thumb is to dress so you wouldn't be embarrassed to meet a woman or business contact for lunch.

2. Confident men make goals and keep them. Goals are promises we make to ourselves.

3. Exercise. Nothing boosts confidence more than exercise. The increased blood flow makes you feel good and hormones are released that boost confidence.

4. Learn a new skill. Confident men are constant learners. By learning a new skill, you show yourself that you're capable of adapting to anything life throws at you.

5. Write down past successes in a journal. When you need a confidence boost, look at them. Realizing you can succeed breeds confidence. This is explained more in the next few pages.

⤳ SIMPLE ACTIVITY TO ⤶ BUILD CONFIDENCE

For my son,

If you have ever suffered from lack of confidence, you know it's not a good feeling. It happens if you ever feel "less than" or are unaware of your strengths. The kind of self-esteem that is important to have is a positive feeling about yourself, your ideas, and your worth that enables you to take good care of yourself and feel pride about who you are and how you live your life.

A simple exercise for confidence-building is a "Daily Success Review."[4] This is a cousin to the gratitude journal where you write down what you are grateful for. In this, you focus on three successes, large or small, that you had in a day. Take a couple of minutes or less to make a note of one to three successes of your day.

By focusing on daily wins, you are training your brain and reinforcing constructive, positive actions and thoughts, making it likely you'll have more small wins in the future. To

---

4. Selig, M. "How to Be More Self-Confident in Just 3 Minutes a Day," psychologytoday.com

give you some ideas, here are 10 possible small wins to notice as you go through your day:

1. You made a good decision.

2. You took time to exercise.

3. You made a mistake and learned from it.

4. You felt compassion for yourself when you made a mistake instead of beating yourself up.

5. You responded to a situation in a better way than you normally would.

6. You took a break when you got tired instead of pushing yourself in an unhealthy way.

7. You refrained from making a bad situation worse.

8. You helped someone.

9. You made progress on a project.

10. You did something healthy for your mind such as meditating or doing the Daily Success Review.

Can you think of three successes you've already had today? To see if this will work for you, try it for a few weeks. Feel free to NOT do it sometimes. Your goal is to develop a small-success mindset, so that you can be aware of the many positive things you do each day. You can train your brain to learn to recognize a small success after it occurs. When you notice something good that you do, give yourself an inner compliment, using healthy self-talk like, "Hey, I handled that pretty well!" "Good decision!" "Way to go!"

If you can't seem to find successes in your day, you may be searching too hard for big achievements. Remember the small wins. Given our brain's negative bias, you may also find yourself focusing too much on failures. You can learn from failures too, but if the whole day was one mishap after another, just forgive yourself and move on. Building self-confidence is a process.

This exercise is a great way to get to know yourself. As you do it, you will start to see patterns. You may realize that you have a strength in one area and a weakness in another.

You could notice what you value. You will begin to more easily recognize people, places, and things that lift you up, and people, places, and things that may drag you down. Just thinking about past successes has positive effects on behavior and there is research that suggests recognizing your own successes can raise your IQ 10 points. Training yourself to be able to savor your successes will make your life more pleasant and more meaningful. Since pleasure and meaning are two essential ingredients of happiness, you will feel happier, too. I wish for you all the happiness you desire.

Love,
Mom

NO ONE CAN MAKE YOU FEEL INFERIOR

For my son,

> "Remember no one can make you feel inferior without your consent."
>
> **– Eleanor Roosevelt**

It is easy to blame how we feel on others, but we have a choice in how we feel and how we respond. Next time someone makes you feel small, take a look at yourself and how you reacted to it. You can turn it around and make strength from it. The way you feel is a matter of choice. No one has the power to control the way you feel unless you give that power away to someone else. The question of identity is at the heart of how you feel about yourself. The feelings of superiority and inferiority live in each of us. You decide how you want to feel. The control over response is entirely yours. There is one person who gets to define you . . . YOU!

You have control over the choices you make: the way you think, the way you behave, the way you eat, and how you dress. How you do these can determine not only how you feel about yourself, but how well and how long you live. It's only when you unwillingly or unconsciously give the control of your life and your choices to others that you are controlled by them. Even this choice is yours and yours alone. Feelings of inferiority indicate that a part of that person's identity is hurt, so they feel they are not worthy. Inferiority comes from insecurity. A person who isn't secure and who does not take pride in him or herself is more likely to give consent or the power to others to make themselves feel inferior. Being vulnerable to influence is in your own hands. If someone does not respect themselves, others are less likely to show any respect to them. It begins with you. It is only when you believe what others think that you give consent to others to make you feel the way they want you to feel. You have the power to reject people's preconceived ideas about who you are by being secure and confident in your life, having self-belief, and being honest with yourself. Being and feeling the way you want truly lies in your own hands. The same point was made by Abraham Lincoln,

"No man is good enough to govern another man without the other's consent."
– **Abraham Lincoln**

Find people that make you feel good for who you are, affirm your soul, and are excited about your life and ideas. Learn, grow, and live the life you dreamed.

Love,
Mom

QUOTES TO LIVE BY

"If I have lost confidence in myself, the world is against me."

– Ralph Waldo Emerson

"The distance between try and triumph is a little umph."

– Author Unknown

"Either write something worth reading or do something worth writing."

– Benjamin Franklin

"Fight for things that you care about but do it in a way that will lead others to join you."

– Ruth Bader Ginsburg

"Learn from yesterday, live for today, hope for tomorrow. The important thing is to not stop questioning."

– Albert Einstein

QUOTES TO LIVE BY

"We realize the importance of our voices only when we are silenced."

– Malala Yousafzai

"If you think you can do a thing or think you can't do a thing, you're right. "

– Henry Ford

"Learning never exhausts the mind."

– Leonardo DaVinci

"Don't criticize what you don't understand."

– Bob Dylan

"You gain strength, courage, and confidence by every experience in which you really stop to look fear in the face. You must do the thing you think you cannot do."

– Eleanor Roosevelt

UNWRITTEN SOCIAL RULES
(Author Unknown)

🎋

1. Never kiss a baby that isn't yours.

2. When you call someone two times in a row and they don't answer, stop blowing up their phone. Respect yourself.

3. Cover your mouth when you cough or sneeze.

4. Give the waiter the same respect you give the CEO. How you treat the waiter says a lot about an individual.

5. Don't invade someone else's personal space. Keep a few feet away when talking.

6. Stop being late every time, it's annoying.

7. Call or give someone a heads-up that you aren't going to make it.

8. Mind your own business. Unless something involves you directly just stay out of it.

9. When invited to a party or event, it's rude to bring a plus one without informing the host.

10. Give your roommate a heads-up if you are bringing someone home.

11. Wash your hands and flush the toilet after you finish your business.

12. Don't give sweets or other small gifts to kids you are not related to—people will confuse your motives.

13. Stop bragging and stay humble.

14. Don't be the loudest in a crowd. Weigh the pitch and loudness in the room and keep it around there.

15. When visiting someone's house, never come empty-handed. Bring food, drinks, candy, flowers.

16. When friends are pitching in to buy food or drinks and you don't have money, ask one of them to loan the money to you so that you can contribute.

17. When visiting someone's house, if they have already made food, don't eat the food unless you told them you were coming over. You may spoil their plans.

18. When eating out with friends, talk after you've finished swallowing your food.

19. Go to the end of the line—wait your turn.

20. If you puke in someone's car or house, make sure you get it cleaned. Saying sorry won't clean it.

⊰ MY WISH FOR YOU ⊱

For my son,

> "May you live as long as you wish and love as long as you live."
>
> **– Robert A. Heinlein**

I wish you the strength to face challenges with confidence. I wish that this life becomes all that you want. I wish that your dreams be big and your worries stay small. You never need to carry more than you can hold. Rise up by lifting up others, play fair, and always ask if you need help. There is nothing so strong as a man who can be tender and nothing so weak as a man who has to be tough. We gave you wings so you can soar. Enjoy the ride and don't forget your way home. I believe in you, always have, and always will. I always said one day I would have to let you go. I lied. I'm never letting go.

Love,
Mom

❧ AS YOU BEGIN TO STEP AWAY ❧

For my son,

As you grow up and begin to step away, your dad and I will fade into the background. I want to tell you it has been a privilege and an honor to have you as our son. Your amazing spirit, dedication, brilliant mind, and creative intuition all add up to a future of great potential and promise. There are a few things I think are important to remember as you go forward in your own life.

1. **People are basically good.** A leader's strength is being able to find the goodness in people. If it is hidden, then bring it out to shine. If you can do it even when it's difficult, you will find the best that people have to offer.

2. **There is no finish line.** It's important to have goals, but don't think of them as the "be all" of what you do. Along the way, enjoy the experiences and the journey, as they will become part of you. If you are

constantly pushing for the next ending, you'll miss some fantastic happenings along the way.

3. **Give of yourself and the world will give to you.** Give of yourself in word and action. The only time you should look down on someone is when you are extending a hand to help them up. You are young, strong, and smart. You can change someone's life with quiet support. Be someone's hero—the world needs more of those.

4. **Keep your mind open to new ideas and experiences.** Take care of your body and test its limits. Take chances but don't ever risk your own health or safety on a dare or foolish prank. People do exciting things all the time. When you want to do something outside of your experience, go for it. But . . . research it, find someone who knows how to do it, then learn, practice, and step forward with confidence. The best way to arm yourself for success is to gain knowledge.

5. **Choose your partner wisely.** It is rare that you can change someone with love, so choose wisely as to who you give your heart. If you find that love is causing you to compromise your other values, then examine it closely. Loving someone means your values align and you can see yourself working hard to stay with that person. Even then there are no guarantees. Falling in love is easy. You can fall in love with just about anyone. Find someone worthy of your love and then put in the work that defines a loving relationship. If someone is worth the effort over and over again, you're on the right track.

6. **Never forget that you are loved for who you are right now.** You are not alone in any challenge you undertake. Our family is strong, and regardless of difficulties we have had, we are all here for you when you need support.

7. **Don't give up on the big stuff, don't sweat the small stuff.** It's going to be ok.

Now it's time for you to fly. Enjoy the freedom and the exhilaration of life and learning. It makes me happy to see that in you. Life isn't about waiting for the storm to pass; it's about learning to dance in the rain. You can withstand any storm. I will be there at every turn possible to embrace your successes, support your learning when you make mistakes, and provide you a soft place to land when you need it. You've got this son, and if you need anything, I've got you too.

Love,
Mom

ADVICE NOW THAT YOU'RE AN ADULT

1. Always be kind.

2. Actions speak louder than words. There are always people less fortunate than you. Be a bright spot in someone's day.

3. Save your money.

4. Be mindful of your decisions and actions. Don't get crazy with impulsive or spur-of-the-moment decisions. A little spontaneity is good. Rushing into important decisions, not so much.

5. Your word is everything.

6. Love is a verb.

7. Always respect your friends and family.

8. Use credit cards wisely. Credit cards can be a useful tool but can cause a lot of damage if misused.

9. When tough times hit, be the eye of the hurricane, the calm part in the middle of the storm.

10. Never forget your parents love you with their entire hearts and souls

QUOTES TO LIVE BY

"Do what you can, where you are, with what you have."

– Theodore Roosevelt

"Dreaming, after all, is a form of planning."

– Gloria Steinem

"The weak can never forgive. Forgiveness is the attribute of the strong."

– Mahatma Gandhi

"It is not the strongest or the most intelligent who will survive but those who can best manage change."

– Charles Darwin

"The world is a dangerous place to live. Not because of the people who are evil, but because of the people who don't do anything about it."

– Albert Einstein

QUOTES TO LIVE BY

"You cannot shake hands
with a clenched fist."
– Indira Gandhi

"Work like you don't need the money, love
like you've never been hurt, and dance like
nobody's watching."
– Satchel Paige

"How wonderful it is that nobody need
wait a single moment before starting to
improve the world."
Anne Frank

"The pessimist sees difficulty in
every opportunity. The optimist sees
opportunity in every difficulty."
– Winston Churchill

"Life without love is like a tree without
blossoms or fruit."
– Khalil Gibran

10 THINGS I NEVER TOLD YOU

1. I always put you first.

2. You made me cry . . . a lot.

3. I'm not perfect.

4. I watched you sleep.

5. You kept me up at night.

6. It broke my heart every time you were hurt or cried.

7. I carried you . . . a lot.

8. I got hit and spit up on.

9. I made a lot of food for you.

10. I would do it all over again.

RULES FOR SONS
(Author Unknown)

1. Never shake a man's hand sitting down.

2. Act like you've been there before.

3. The man at the grill is the closest thing to a king.

4. In a negotiation, never make the first offer.

5. Request the late check out.

6. When entrusted with a secret, keep it.

7. Hold your heroes to a higher standard.

8. Play with passion. . . or not at all.

9. Return a borrowed car with a full tank of gas.

10. Don't fill up on bread.

11. When shaking hands, grip firmly with eye contact.

12. Don't let a wishbone grow where a backbone should be.

13. Carry two handkerchiefs. The one in your back pocket is for you. The one in your breast pocket is for her.

14. Be like a duck. Remain calm on the surface and paddle like crazy underneath.

15. Never be afraid to ask out the best looking girl in the room.

16. Never turn down a breath mint.

17. A sport coat is worth a thousand words.

18. Try writing your own eulogy. Never stop revising.

19. Thank a veteran. And then make it up to him/her.

20. Eat lunch with the new kid.

21. After writing an angry email, read it carefully, then delete.

22. Ask your mom to play. She won't let you win.

23. Manners make the man.

24. Give credit, take the blame.

25. Stand up to bullies. Protect those that are bullied.

26. Write down your dreams.

27. Always protect your family, friends, and your teammates.

28. Be confident and humble at the same time.

29. Call and visit your parents. They miss you.

30. The healthiest relationships are those where you are a team; where you respect, protect, and stand up for each other.

⤙ THIS I BELIEVE ⤚

This I Believe was a five-minute CBS Radio Network program hosted by journalist Edward R. Murrow from 1951 to 1955. My grandfather, your great grandfather, H. Fred Heisner, wrote this essay for broadcast.[5]

In the first place, I believe everyone is important. This is a faith, and although there are probably reasonable arguments to support this idea, I think it is an appreciation that has become stronger over the years as I have come to know people. I am struck by the fact that we all have the same fundamental human feelings, and it is impossible for any of us to think of ourselves as completely unimportant, and live.

The next belief which follows from this is that the most important job for each is the fulfillment of human personality. Each person has a place, and each can become a personality. In a way, there is inside each of us a blueprint of what each can become. This becoming transcends all other human aims. We become persons as we relate to others. Jesus and other

---

5. "This I Believe," H. Fred Heisner, 1950s.

teachers saw that we must relate ourselves to others through love. All of us are aware that this at times seems almost impossible. I believe that it is fear that keeps us from loving our neighbor. "Perfect love casteth out fear," the Apostle Paul tells us, but fear also casts out love. If we are to help each person develop his potentialities, it is important that we minimize fear.

In spite of the difficulties, however, I believe a satisfying life is possible. Our real satisfactions will come in, about, the proportion we are able to achieve the personality that God intended. This does not mean that we'll be happy, as happiness is often superficially defined. Trouble is everywhere, and part of our development will depend on our ability to face trouble. My own troubles have often come with shocking suddenness. As a junior in college, I was called home because my youngest sister, a girl of 13, was dying. More recently, I was shocked when the doctors diagnosed my son's difficulties as muscular dystrophy. These and other troubles have convinced me that personality fulfillment is not dependent upon length of life but on its quality. Our personalities can be fulfilled for any given time in life or for any condition.

Personality fulfillment is for each day. My son, who is now confined to a wheelchair, demonstrates this to us. His fine, cheery relationships with everyone is an inspiration to all who know him. Trouble can make us cynical and bitter, or it can build new bonds with our fellows, for the person without trouble is rare. Trouble is only one of the challenges to our development. Another is a person with whom a relationship of love seems impossible. There seems to be an urge in each toward self-realization. Even though true self-realization comes through a love relationship, many people because of their experiences exhibit hostility. When people seem to be mean or thoughtless, we can only hope that we can help them get more insight into life. If we believe that the nature of man thrives on love and this is what God intends for us, we must go a step further and trust that this truth will prevail. If we can understand this, it is because of our experiences. If we can help others have similar experiences, this insight will develop in them too.

As a teacher, I find ways to work for these beliefs in an organized way. I am sure that similar opportunities exist in all professions. I believe that peace and happiness in the world depends on universal acceptance of these principles.

QUOTES TO LIVE BY

"Emancipate yourself from mental
slavery, none but ourselves
can free our mind."

– Bob Marley

"A champion is afraid of losing.
Everyone else is afraid of winning."

– Billie Jean King

"Words may show a man's wit,
actions its meaning."

– Benjamin Franklin

"Happiness is a continuation of
happenings which are not resisted."

– Deepak Chopra

"What we achieve inwardly will
change outer reality."

– Plutarch

QUOTES TO LIVE BY

"Do not let what you cannot do interfere with what you can."
– John Wooden

"Your mind will answer most questions if you learn to relax and wait for the answer."
– William S. Burroughs

"Love is the beauty of the soul."
– St Augustine

"Only surround yourself with people who can lift you higher."
– Oprah Winfrey

"There are many languages in the world. A smile speaks all of them."
– Anonymous

⊰ YOU ARE THE GIFT ⊱

For my son,

> "Yesterday is history, tomorrow is a mystery. Today is a gift, that's why they call it the present."
> **– Alice Morse Earle**

You are the gift. Focus on the present. The past is unchangeable, so it is useless to reflect on unless you are making sure not make the same mistakes again. We never stop making mistakes, but hopefully we learn from them and don't make the same mistake twice. The future is a result of your actions today. So, learn from the past to do better in the present so you can succeed in the future.

Love,
Mom

⊰ KARMA ⊱

For my son,

Karma is a fundamental part of life and it applies to everyone regardless of belief. Have you ever heard someone say, "What goes around, comes around" or "He got what was coming to him"?

Karma means that the sum of a person's actions decides their fate.

How do we earn good karma?

- Be positive
- Show self-respect and respect for others
- Take responsibility for your actions
- Offer forgiveness
- Correct your mistakes
- Share knowledge
- Be compassionate
- Search for wisdom
- Spread love and harmony
- Follow your inherent nature and perform your passions

Karma is a universal law, not a choice. Believe in it. Every living being abides by this law. The intention behind it is more important than the act itself. Suffering and happiness are related to karma. Negative actions lead to suffering and positive actions result in happiness. If you know this, then you already believe in karma. Sometimes it may take what seems like a lifetime for the realization of karmic results. The timing isn't for you to decide. Remember, every soul has a purpose. Only through performing acts of good karma through positive intentions can we ultimately achieve happiness and peace. I wish you peace and happiness always.

Love,
Mom

✢ YOUR IMAGINATION ✥ IS YOUR PREVIEW

For my son,

> "Your imagination is your preview of life's coming attractions."
>
> **— Albert Einstein**

Imagine for a moment that you have the power to bring anything into your life your heart desires. Imagine that there are no limits and it's impossible to fail. What would you choose to do? Go ahead, take a moment and capture that image in your mind. So what is preventing you from accomplishing that goal? Consider your heart's desires today and evaluate the real stumbling blocks that stand in your way. Brainstorm ways to overcome them and set short-term goals that lead you in the direction of your dreams. You have a sturdy foundation of love and education to propel you forward to something wonderful. You are made from love and your heart is golden. You are a bright light that grows and can illuminate the lives of others. Your gifts need to be shared with the world.

One of my fondest memories is when we were in the Grand Canyon and you were so eager to earn your Junior Ranger badge. You were amazing to watch; so passionate, creative, and excited to learn everything you possibly could. It was inspiring to watch you be so curious with an amazing yearning for learning. Don't ever lose that. You are a beautiful soul that loves nature and animals, just like my father, your Grandpa Ben. I wish he was here to see what a remarkable human you have become. You even smell like him. I know it sounds odd, but then it doesn't, because you are a part of him.

Your Grandpa Ben was the first person in his family to get a college education. It takes a lot of determination and courage to create your own path, one different from those around you. You have the same resolve to forge your own path. Nothing is more tranquil to the mind than a steady goal toward your desired path.

Sometimes your path may take an unforeseen detour like when your Grandpa Ben was drafted into WWII at the age of 18. This forever altered the direction of his life. What he saw in the war changed him and, in turn, the stories he told about the war shaped me. He utilized the GI Bill to get his education. GI Bill benefits provided educational and housing opportunities for millions of veterans. He attended the University of Nevada and then received a scholarship for his graduate studies from Stanford University where he met my mother, your grandmother. One could say you are a product of Stanford University, and so am I (see articles next page). He earned his doctorate degree, a dream that your Great Grandfather Harrison shared with his son. Ben made his dreams a reality and you can do the same. Stay true to yourself, but always be open to learn. I know you can do whatever you set your heart and mind to do.

Love,
Mom

❧ STANFORD ENGAGEMENT ❧

Engagement Of Marilyn Heisner Announced

Announcement was made on Stanford university campus last Sunday by Marilyn Frances Heisner, who graduates tomorrow, of her engagement to Ben Banta of Reno, Nevada.

Marilyn is the daughter of Dr. and Mrs. H. Fred Heisner, 213 Roma street, Redlands, and granddaughter of Mr. and Mrs. Frank S. Gunter, 1018 Campus avenue. Her father is superintendent of schools for Redlands and her grandfather is a former mayor and civic leader here. Marilyn graduated from Inglewood High school and has studied for four years at Stanford.

Her fiance, son of the late Mr. and Mrs. Harrison A. Banta, is a graduate of the University of Nevada and is currently completing studies for his Ph. D. in biological science at Stanford.

Engagement of my parents, your grandparents
Redlands Daily Facts - 06-15 -1957, used by permission

⤐ WEDDING ⥽

Wedding of my parents, your grandparents
Redlands Daily Facts - 09-07-1957, used by permission

❧ BEING YOUR PARENT ❧

For my son,

Being your parent has been one of the greatest gifts in my life. It's difficult to describe how much I love you, and there is nothing that could ever change how I feel. I will never forget those cherished moments of you as a young boy, like each time you saw the first star at night you would look up to the sky, clasp your hands together tightly, and make a hopeful wish. You always wished for something inspirational, beautiful, or creative for the world and the people around you. You are a beautiful soul with so much to offer. You deserve to be happy and live a life you are excited about. Don't let anyone let you forget that.

**Love,
Mom**

❦ I CLOSED MY EYES ❧ FOR A MOMENT

Photo by Colleen Morgans, used by permission

For my son,

It seems like I closed my eyes for a moment and suddenly a man stood where a boy used to be. I may not carry you now in my arms, but I will always carry you in my heart. You have given me so many reasons to be proud of the man you have become, but the proudest moment for me is telling others you are my son.

Love,
Mom

SUN

DJ content to do triple time in career choices

by Brad Fichter
Sun Writer

I f you ever meet Meg Banta and ask her what profession she is in, you better have a few minutes to listen for the answer.

Banta could tell you about her radio career. She is an evening disc personality for Carlsbad radio station KKOS FM.

Banta could tell you about her science career. She is what could be called an amateur biologist whose interests put her in studying reptiles and marine life.

Banta also could tell you about her video career. Wearing that hat, she recently was honored by the San Diego Chapter of the National Association of Television Arts and Sciences during the Emmy Awards ceremony June 10.

"You could say I am many," said Banta, 25, who holds a degree in television and film from San Diego State University. "I too decide what I want

to do because I love what I'm doing. Maybe that was too strong. Banta's life is by what pays the bills. Her paying job is as a radio jockey. She is the host of a show from 7 p.m. to midnight.

Meg Banta looks quite comfortable in her job as an evening radio personality on Carlsbad station KKOS. Staff photo/Kim Brooks

"It's a request show," said Banta, who is a native of Solana Beach. "We play adult album alternative music. I love talking to people doing that."

Banta's love of biology was passed down from her father, Ben, who she said for years has led trips to the Sea of

Cortez in Mexico to study reptiles.

"I love going along with my father," said Banta. "It is so interesting."

So interesting that Banta decided to chronicle the Sea of Cortez in a video. She wrote, produced, directed and narrated the video titled "A Voyage to the Sea of

Cortez."

"I worked on it for two years," said Banta. "I wanted to do a project that was me. I love the area. It is so removed from buildings and people. On our last trip, we had killer whales low riding the boat."

Banta got the idea to enter the video in the contest from a friend Roger Dopp. She also took much of the inspiration for the video from Lester Knapp, a professor at Palomar College who shared her love for the Sea of

Cortez. Both Dopp and Knapp passed away before the video was finished.

"I dedicated it to them," said Banta as her voice trailed off.

Banta isn't sure what direction she'll head in the future. But unless she gets a job offer from, say the Discovery Channel making videos, she said she'll probably continue her multiple-profession life.

"I'm happy," said Banta. "That's what matters."

The Carlsbad Sun, June 29, 1995, used with permission

ABOUT THE AUTHOR

Meg Ford is a retired Professor of Media Studies specializing in radio broadcasting, for which she has written two books. Meg worked professionally in the broadcast industry for over 25 years. A graduate of San Diego State University, Meg (Banta) has been heard throughout the San Diego radio market on stations like KPRI, KKOS, KCEO, KXST, 91X, XTRA 690AM, and KPBS. Meg earned an Emmy award for the documentary "A Voyage to the Sea of Cortez" which she produced, directed, and narrated. She also narrated the Telly award winning documentary, "A World of Autism." Meg Ford now spends her time working on projects with meaning, such as this book, *For My Son*, inspired by her own son becoming a man and the letters she wrote to him in a journal for his eighteenth birthday. Meg is honored to be the mother of two amazing children, Tyler and Rachel.

28471836R00078

Made in the USA
San Bernardino, CA
07 March 2019